Simple
Elegant
Flowers

Simple
Elegant
Flowers

Avril O'Donnell

Over 30 ideas for stylish arrangements

NEW HOLLAND

To Isabella

Published in 2007 by
New Holland Publishers (UK) Ltd
London • Cape Town • Sydney • Auckland
www.newhollandpublishers.com

Garfield House
86-88 Edgware Road
London W2 2EA
United Kingdom

80 McKenzie Street
Cape Town 8001
South Africa

14 Aquatic Drive
Frenchs Forest, NSW 2086
Australia

218 Lake Road
Northcote, Auckland
New Zealand

ISBN 978 1 84537 729 8

Editor: Ruth Hamilton
Designer: Ian Sandom
Photographer: Stuart West
Photographic stylist: Avril O'Donnell
Production: Hazel Kirkman
Editorial direction: Rosemary Wilkinson

10 9 8 7 6 5 4 3 2 1

Reproduction by Pica Digital PTE Ltd, Singapore
Printed and bound by Times Offset (M) Sdn Bhd, Malaysia

Contents

Introduction

This book is not just about flower arranging in its conventional form, it is about using flowers in different ways to produce attractive displays around the home and for any occasion. The way in which this is achieved is by careful selection of which flowers to put together and what type of container they are placed in to show them off to their best advantage.

Using flowers in the home will bring colour and beauty to wherever you choose to put them. In every season there is a huge range of flowers to pick from in all colours, shapes and sizes. From the traditional to the more exotic varieties, all blooms are now more readily available than ever before, thanks to specialist growers all over the world.

Some of the most effective displays are often the most simple, both in choice of flower and container, whether you are just picking flowers from your garden or buying cut flowers. When beginning to arrange the flowers, take a good look at the shape and size of the container as this will give you a good indication as to the height and

general shape of the flowers. As a rough guide your arrangement should be approximately one and a half times the height of the container, although I must add there are no hard and fast rules, and you must do whatever you feel looks right.

I hope as you look through this book it will give you plenty of ideas to use flowers as I have done but also to interpret them in your own way by changing flowers and containers to suit the seasons and availability.

Handy information

When creating flower displays you want them to last as long as possible and to show them off to their best advantage with a suitable container. The following advice is essential to perfecting your arrangements.

When buying fresh flowers look out for good quality blooms which have healthy leaves and petals which are either just open or about to open. Re-cut the stems at an angle with a sharp pair of scissors when you get them home, and remove any lower leaves and shoots that will be below the water line. Make sure that the water you place them in is not too cold as this can be a shock to the flowers.

When picking flowers or greenery from the garden try to pick them either in the morning or evening as this is the time when they hold the most water. As with bought flowers, cut the stems at an angle as this will alllow them to take in the maximum amount of water. Place them in water as soon as possible.

To make sure your displays last as long as possible, use flower food where available and change the water regularly so it doesn't start to smell or get cloudy. Take any dead flowers or leaves off when necessary and re-cut stems and rinse them under the tap to keep your flowers fresh for longer.

Each project has individual advice about suitable containers, but there are a few general tips to try and follow. The first is to keep in mind the size of flowers and arrangement you are creating, and to make sure the flowers are not too heavy for the vase or that the flowers are so small they are lost in the container. Consider where you want to put your arrangement and make sure the container fits; a display for a shelf can't be too deep and a table display shouldn't be so tall that you can't see over the top of it. When using containers that aren't traditional vases, make sure that they are fully waterproof. If you are not sure then line with plastic or place a glass container inside as a precaution.

FAST FLOWERS

This chapter is full of displays that can be used for any occasion, whether you want something special for a dinner party or to simply brighten up your home. The use of flowers around the home needn't be restricted to formal arrangements; using very easy ideas you can bring colour and vibrance to a room throughout the year. The following displays are all simple to achieve and quick to do, giving maximum impact for minimum effort.

Potty about baskets

I have found that such simple items as flower pots and baskets make great and effective containers. They can be old or new, but you will need to put a waterproof lining in, as terracotta pots and baskets are porous. This could be as simple as placing a glass inside the pot.

Use a selection of large and small containers together, arranged in a nice shape where you want them to be. One or two could even be placed lying on their side.

In the larger pots you can use all sorts of flowers and greenery. Put them in bunches by tying them with string and popping them into glasses inside the pots. This will also help the flowers stand up straight in the pots.

In the smaller flower pots use flowers such as pansies, lily of the valley, daisies or grape hyacinths.

Flowers used in photography: delphiniums and lavender

Big and bold

Arrangements can be any size, it really depends on how much space you have. This is a suggestion for a large display, perhaps for a fireplace or an alcove.

In this particular instance I have used an old wooden box with individual containers or vases placed within the box to make it easier when you put the flowers in.

This is a great opportunity to use lots of lovely greenery to fill out the space, remember to look around your garden or surrounding green areas to help fill the box. Gradually build up the foliage, you may need to add more containers as you continue.

Place flowers in groups for maximum colour. With a display like this the variety of foliage and flowers is almost endless, so use whatever you have available. Use a piece of wood (such as bamboo stick) to prop the lid open to the best height.

Flowers used in photography: sedum, variegated ivy, hydrangea, Russian vine

English garden

A more informal type of arrangement, this idea comes from the old fashioned cottage garden. An old watering can has been used to great effect for this type of display. Other less conventional containers may also be used so have a look around the garden or shed for inspiration.

The idea of this very informal display is for you to use flowers and foliage from the garden. Flowers that are always good to use are any type of roses, peonies or lupines.

Start by using the main flowers, place them in roughly the shape you feel suits the container. Continue by filling in the spaces in between, keep looking all around the arrangement to get the shape that you like.

Now fill in any gaps you have with foliage. Add lots of greenery, big leaves, branches or trailing foliage and allow it to be uneven and flowing.

Flowers used in photography:
antique roses, wild angelica

Kitchen delights

Looking around the kitchen I have found several interesting containers which could be utilized as flower containers. Suggestions include sugar bowls, utensil holders or even old saucepans. I have chosen to use jars as these come in so many shapes and sizes.

Wash out the containers thoroughly and soak off any labels you do not want, but if they have interesting labels it might be nice to leave them on. If the jars have flip top lids this is not a problem just incorporate the feature into the display.

Fill with brightly coloured flowers that look natural and a bit wild, for example cornflowers, honeysuckle or sweetpeas. Use bits of greenery from the garden like clematis, leaves or ivy.

To add a different dimension try filling with lovely fresh herbs such as rosemary, thyme and chives.

Flowers used in photography: sweet peas, heather, rosemary, ivy, wild angelica

Tanks and leaves

This idea is not actually about using flowers! It is about using foliage and choosing different shapes of leaves in various shades of green. This is a great way of creating cool smart displays for any room.

Use a selection of glass vases and tanks, choose different sizes and shapes, and make sure they are all sparkling clean. Place the vases where you want to display them and fill them with varying levels of water.

Now pick a selection of different shaped leaves and place them in the containers in different ways. Some may be tall with most of the leaf coming out of the vase, others may be completely contained within the tank. The most important thing is to look at the group as a whole and see which elements make the best composition. To add further interest you could put some stones or large pebbles in the bottom of one or two of the tanks.

Leaves used in photography: cheese plant leaf, fern, eucalyptus, bells of Ireland

Green and fruity

Continuing on a green theme, create some tall impressive displays using large glass vases. Fill with structurally shaped foliage in cool shades of green.

To make these displays more striking place some fruit in the bottom of the vase. This could be apples, pears, or to add another colour, maybe oranges or lemons.

Fill the vase with enough water to cover most of the fruit and still allow enough for the stems of the foliage to sit in it.

Choose your greenery and place in the vase. Remember to pick nice tall long leaves or branches as these will help balance the display. Remember that you will have to change the fruit regularly so that it doesn't go off and ruin the display.

Flowers used in photography: phormium leaves, sword fern, still grass, eremurus (foxtail lily)

Pretty tiny

As this title suggests this project is about using small containers and blooms.
You can use glasses, cups or simply tiny vases if you have any.

For this example I am using tea light holders. They look particularly good on shelves or a mantelpiece if you use two or three together.

These can be new or old, if they have been used make sure you wash out any old wax. This can be done by firstly cleaning with white spirit then washing with hot soapy water.

Fill small containers with little flowers such as daisies, tiny bud roses or grape hyacinths, alternatively you could use a single larger flower. Remember to take into consideration the size of the flowers, you don't want anything too large which will overpower the container.

Flowers used in photography:
wild dog-rose

Just blossoms

Using blossoms in the spring is a beautiful way of bringing a touch of changing seasons into your home. From large branches to single blooms, this type of arrangement can look stunning.

Choose blossoms that are in bud rather than fully blooming, mainly because if cut later they will shed their petals too quickly. Common varieties easily found are apple blossom and cherry blossom, or you could use something slightly different like forsythia or magnolia.

Pick shapely large glass vases and make sure they are sparkling clean. Use long branches of blossoms to fill the space. It may help to use something like stones or glass pebbles to weight the bottom as using tall branches can make the display top heavy.

If you have a narrow necked vase, using just one branch is particularly effective. Or if you are lucky enough to have a magnolia tree in your garden try just using a couple of the single flowers in low glasses.

Flowers used in photography:
kangaroo paw

Green and flowering

When it comes to making a worthwhile display it does not come any simpler than using differing types of shrubs such as lilac, hydrangea, hebes and viburnum – all of these have wonderful leaves and fantastic flowers at certain times of the year.

These type of shrubs can of course be used in many different ways. Something that works well is a good heavy clay pot or ceramic vase. You could also use a glass jug as I have done.

Taking the container you have chosen, simply fill with branches, so that it is almost brimming over.

Make sure you remember to take all the lower leaves and flowers off below the water line, so the display stays fresh for as long as possible.

Flowers used in photography: hydrangeas

Twigs and things

Although we have not used flowers, this is a good way of introducing different shapes and textures into your displays. Used on their own twigs such as tortured willow and catkins can make a very graphic modern display.

The type of vase or container you use is very important with this type of display as the twigs are very simple, therefore the choice of vessel needs to make a statement.

A nice idea to enhance these displays is to decorate them, this can be done with hanging crystals that catch the light, or by using something pretty such as beads, threads or ribbons.

Finally, adding flowers would give extra colour and softness to a display. Only one or two are needed; perhaps something like gerberas or lilies which will give a lovely splash of vibrancy.

Twigs used in photography:
tortured willow

Simply stylish

To make this arrangement a little different use grass decorated with some beads as a simple eye-catcher. For a clean sophisticated look try choosing a smoked glass vase with modern simple lines that will enhance any room.

Use some greenery, such as bear grass and place in to the vase. Allow them to bend over and touch the surface, you may need to cut them at the base.

Beads can be added by slipping them on to the pointed ends of the grasses, it may be necessary to cut the points a little thinner to make it easier.

Complete this elegant display by carefully adding a few specially selected flowers, such as calla or arum lilies, orchids or even a few tulips, to the vase.

Flowers used in photography:
calla lilies, bear grass

Hanging around

There are so many different types of vases available these days so it is nice to come across something a little unusual. In this instance I have used a vase which doesn't even need a surface to stand on as it is designed to hang.

The first thing to think about is where to put a hanging vase. Make sure that it will be safe and not where it can be knocked; maybe next to a fireplace or hanging from the end of a curtain pole.

Choose trailing types of greenery, as it will look fantastic spilling out of the vase, and delicate flowers such as scabious, clary, or maybe Bells of Ireland to add another texture.

Try starting with trailing greenery: ivy, vine or whatever you find that will come out of the vase and flow down its length. Then put your selected flowers in. Allow plenty of space around the flowers so the arrangement does not look too cramped.

Flowers used in photography: scabious, jasmine, bells of Ireland

Single stems

Using only one or two stems of flowers and foliage is flower arranging at its most basic and most stunning. Choosing containers is just as important here as the choices of flower, because the type of container or vase will dictate which sort of flower you can use.

Generally vases with narrow necks suit single stems as they sit better in these, however simple glasses like tumblers can be just as effective.

Using multiple containers is a good way to add impact to this type of display although you may decide that keeping it simple with one vase works as well.

Types of flower you can use here are extremely varied. Some of the obvious are gerberas, roses, delphiniums, sunflowers, orchids, lilies and peonies, but you can use anything with a pretty flower head and fairly long stems.

Flowers used in photography:
scabious

Naturally earthy

For this theme I have chosen a lovely banana wood vase in warm shades of brown and beige. This will lend itself to a lovely natural arrangement using soft foliage in shades of green and brown, adding flowers such as love in a mist, larkspur or snapdragon.

Position the vase where you want to display it. Start by putting the greenery in, use the larger pieces first as this will help you create the size and shape quite quickly. Then build up the arrangement by adding flowers.

Remember to remove all leaves going in to the neck of the vase and also below the water line. This will allow the foliage not only to live longer but will also give you more room for the flowers.

You could also use trailing foliage which flows out of the neck and down onto the surface incorporating it into the display. Adding one or two pieces of fruit amongst the trailing foliage would really add to the natural feel of the arrangement.

Flowers used in photography: cotinus (smoke bush), branches of plum, sedum (autumn glory), branches of cherries

Headlines

For this type of arrangement there are no special types of vase needed, the only things required are some simple glass tumblers. The variety of flowers used should have a nice open and fairly even head, such as chrysanthemums, dahlias, carnations or open roses.

First measure the height of the tumbler you use, the flower stems should be cut just shorter than the tumbler.

How many individual flower stems you need depends on how big the heads are and how wide the glasses are. The idea is that the heads should just rest on the lip of the glass, so two or three should be enough.

Arrange the glasses in whatever configuration you like and pop the flower heads in (the heads should all be roughly the same height).

Flowers used in photography: chrysanthemums

Turning Japanese

There are so many different styles of arrangements that are influenced by countries and their cultures. This particular one is from Japan.

Cool uncluttered lines are key in this particular design. A typical shape for a Japanese style arrangement is a low round shape with a narrow neck.

There are particular types of flowers which suit this theme, but the orchid family, the twisted stem of ornithogalum and also anthodium do look especially good. These are all very structural, graphic shapes.

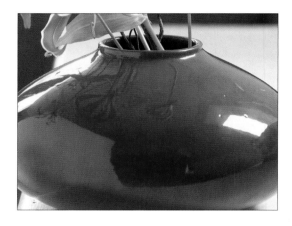

Usually two or three stems are enough for this type of display. Place them to one side of the vase rather than placing them in symmetrically. To add a different texture, try using some tortured willow mixed in with the flowers. To ensure the flowers and foliage stand up neatly, put a piece of florist's foam in the bottom of the vase and insert the stems carefully.

Flowers used in photography: gloriosa lilies, tortured willow

Asian colour

Rich colours of red, gold and orange coupled with exotically shaped vases give this display a truly rich and opulent feel of the Far East. For this design I have chosen two stunning vases which look great grouped together.

Simple bold exotic flowers complement the vase shapes and added texture and colour can be gained through long grasses and willow.

Allow the willow to fall out of the vase in a dramatic way. If the necks of your vases are particularly narrow use grasses that can be wrapped around the flower stems instead.

Suitable flowers for an Oriental look are bird-of-paradise flowers, tall moth orchids or irises.

Flowers used in photography:
bird-of-paradise flowers, willow, still grass

Exotic flavour

For something that is exciting, colourful and a little different, try using a large bowl filled with water and float some bright coloured flower heads in the water. This is a wonderfully flamboyant display which would look great on a low coffee table or as a centre piece on a dining table.

For this particular arrangement I have used a large coloured glass bowl which you might ordinarily put fruit in. To add an exotic touch place some shells in the bottom. Alternatively you could use shiny pebbles or coloured glass beads.

Carefully cut the heads off the flowers you have selected, you will need to leave about a centimetre of the stem to allow the flower to take water. Choose heads which are open, or almost open, and place these in the water.

Try to choose flowers that match the colour of the bowl, but there are lots of different types of flowers you could use, such as stargazer lilies, anemones, peonies or roses. To add a different texture try putting the odd leaf in.

Flowers used in photography: hydrangea

Light fantastic

This particular display has been inspired by the strings of neon and fairy lights which are currently so popular. They add a new dimension to a simple display, and are very effective at nighttime.

When considering where to put the display the important thing to remember is that the lights, if they are mains operated, need to be within reach of a power source, although battery lights are also available. You also need to be careful to keep the wire away from water at all times.

Start by winding the string of lights around the vase, go from top to bottom then fix the string with some tape at the top. Alternatively you may want to just allow the lights to sit around the base of the vase in a cluster.

Choose white flowers to accentuate the look of this arrangement, simply place them in the vase and allow to look fairly natural. Remember to be careful when adding water as you do not want to wet the area around the lights.

Flowers used in photography:
fountain grass, white hydrangeas

Caught in a net

This stunning display is an explosion of colour and style. Choose brightly coloured fabric and flowers to match this display, which will brighten up any dark corner.

The idea of this arrangement is very simple and easy to achieve. It is also a good way of utilizing a container or vase which you may not like any more or it might just be a shape which is no longer fashionable.

Take a length of fabric (I have used yellow netting) about a metre long and fasten it to the bottom of the vase with tape. Now start to wrap it around the vase in a fairly loose fashion, continue to the top and again fasten the end.

Now add your chosen blooms. For maximum impact I have chosen the same colour as the fabric. Use something that has a nice big head like dahlias, sunflowers or peonies. Use as many as it takes to fill out to the edge of the fabric.

Flowers used in photography: double sunflowers

Bottle it!

A good alternative to using conventional glass vases is to use bottles. There are usually plenty around in different shapes and colours. These will look great either in groups or lined up on a shelf or window sill. Choose bottles in all shapes and sizes to get a truly eclectic look.

Take the bottles of your choice and clean them out with hot water, making sure they are fully rinsed. Remove any unwanted labels by soaking them off. Fill the bottles to the halfway level with water and then add the flowers of your choice. In this case one or two stems are enough depending on the flower.

There are two ways of treating this type of display; either you use exactly the same flower in each bottle and have a repetition display, or you can use different flowers in each to vary the shape and texture.

I would suggest things like gerberas, alliums or maybe ranunculus for repetition and perhaps catmint, delphiniums or love in a mist for shape and texture.

Flowers used in photography:
golden rod, scabious

Hats off

It is surprising what you can use as an interesting container, and this is exactly that. A hat which has been given a new lease of life as a vase!

Firstly you need to find an old hat, it doesn't really matter about condition or style, in fact if it is tatty this will only add to the charm.

Turn the hat upside down and find a bowl which fits into it. Remember you will not see the bowl so it can be any old bowl as long as it fits.

Simply fill literally to the brim with flowers! Ideal varieties to use are sunflowers, fluffy carnations, dahlias or anything with a nice big flower head. Use this arrangement as inspiration for using other surprising items found in the home as vases.

Flowers used in photography: sunflowers

THREE STEPS TO STYLISH FLOWERS

The ideas in this chapter are slightly more advanced, but will still give you fabulous results in a short amount of time. There are lots of new and exciting ways to make flowers look fantastic and they do not need to be overcomplicated or fussy Look out for new methods, unusual flowers and inventive containers to push the boundaries of your imagination.

Moss bowl

This lovely display is particularly good for dinner parties as a central piece because it is fairly low. Use a mixture of flowers and greenery which are in season at the time you want to create the arrangement.

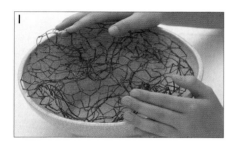

1 Take your bowl, this can be any shape or size, glass or ceramic. Get some wire mesh (from a good garden centre) which is big enough to more than cover the top of the bowl. Shape the mesh to fit inside the bowl below the rim.

2 Now you either need to buy some moss or find some (often found growing in shady areas of lawn or woodland). Cover the mesh with the moss, poking it into some of the holes; allow it to spill over the edges of the bowl.

3 Start to put the flowers into the bowl by poking them through the mesh. You will find that because the moss creates a good cover you will not need to fill every gap. Finally, fill the bowl with water.

Flowers used in photography:
white roses, moss

Leaf tank

An effective way of changing the look of a glass tank is by lining it with lovely glossy leaves. These could be anything from laurel leaves which you may have in the garden to something more tropical which you will find in a florist shop.

1 Use the vase of your choice, the only thing to note is that the neck must not be too narrow. Cut some wet florist's foam to fit inside the vase making sure it goes from top to bottom, but allow a gap between the foam and glass.

2 Remove the foam and begin putting the leaves around the bottom of the vase. Work your way up, covering all areas of glass; it is best to overlap the leaves to make sure there are no holes. When you are a quarter of the way up put the foam back in to help keep the leaves in place. Now soak the foam.

3 To complete the display take some lovely tall agapanthus, or maybe arum lilies, and put them in a tight group in the centre of the foam. To finish place some leaves in the top of the vase.

Flowers used in photography:
variegated laurel leaves, agapanthus

Ring a ring of roses

This simple modern arrangement could work well as a table piece or simply placed on a shelf or mantelpiece.

1 Use some nice tall tumbler glasses, you can do two or three or a whole collection if you want. Choose whichever colour of rose you like, as long as they are long stemmed. Remove any leaves low down on the stems and bunch the roses together so that they fit quite tightly into the tumblers.

2 Now tie the bunches near the top of the stems, use coloured ribbon, raffia or twine. Place the tumblers where they will be displayed and fill them with water.

3 Tuck moss tightly around the base of the roses to keep them in place and add a neat finishing touch.

Flowers used in photography:
long stemmed roses, moss

Grass loops

This is a modern design full of colour and texture which will grace any room. I have chosen a tall modern vase to show off the cage on top but you can adapt this idea to suit most shapes of vase. Roses, dahlias and even chrysanthemums will suit this display.

1 Fill the vase with water and cut a piece of florist's foam to fit into the top of the vase, make sure it is a nice tight fit so it does not fall down into the vase. Wet the foam before you start the arrangement.

2 Before putting the flowers in make sure all the leaves below the flower head have been removed. Start to place the flowers you have chosen into the foam, it does not matter if they go through to the water. Completely cover the area of foam with flower heads.

3 Now, using long still grass, push the blunt end into the foam underneath the flower heads, loop it over the flowers and push the other end in under the opposite flower head. If you feel the grass is too long simply cut it to the length you want. Repeat this process as many times as it takes to loop over the whole display.

Flowers used in photography: anemones, still grass

Tree bark vases

Inspired by woodland walks, this unusual arrangement looks simple and natural. It is also a good way of using old tree bark which normally would rot away into the ground. Flowers such as honeysuckle and wild roses both look lovely in this display.

1 When searching for bark, look for dead branches which have been on the ground for some time as this makes the bark easier to remove. Look for smaller branches where the bark goes all the way around the branch to form a circle and remove it carefully.

2 Trim the base of the bark straight so it will stand up, you may need to wet the bark if it is very brittle. You will need a container to fit inside the curled bark and this will depend on the size of bark you have. I have used glasses that simply sit inside.

3 Arrange the vases in a group. Put the water into the glasses and place the flowers into the vases. Try to choose flowers and foliage which will look as natural and wild as the bark vases.

Flowers used in photography: gloriosa lilies

Painted tins

This idea continues on the recycling theme but this time I am using old tin cans. Painted in pretty colours these look bright and colourful, and work particularly well outside for an outside party or barbecue.

1 First take a selection of tin cans, wash them out carefully and soak off any old labels. Allow to dry thoroughly before continuing.

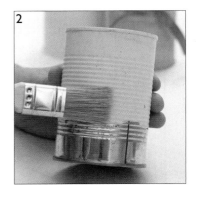

2 There are a couple of ways that you can paint the cans, either by spraying them which you will need to do in a well ventilated area, or by using emulsion paint which will probably need two coats. Either way make sure they are dry before you use them.

3 Now simply place whichever flowers you like into the tins; this can be done in quite a casual way. Use varieties like scabious, lavender, primulas or daffodils, anything that is simple and colourful. Finally, decorate by tying a few matching ribbons around the tins.

Flowers used in photography:
antique roses, scabious, lisianthus

Harvest bunch

Here is an idea for that country cottage feel. It combines golden wheat with fresh flowers and can be used anywhere at any time to decorate your home.

1 Buy lots of lovely wheat for this arrangement (from a good dried flower stockist). Take a straight, fairly tall, plain glass and a couple of elastic bands. Place the bands round the glass, one near the top and the other near the bottom.

2 Cut the wheat to a length longer than the height of the glass. Start to thread the wheat under the bands so that the bottoms of the wheat are in line with the bottom of the glass Continue to put the wheat all the way around the glass until the glass is completely covered.

3 Pick the glass up and twist the wheat so that it fans out slightly at the top. Secure with rough string or raffia. Trim any ends of wheat so that the glass sits on a flat surface, and add your choice of fresh flowers by popping them into the glass of water.

Flowers used in photography: anemones and wheat

Paper roses

This cool, elegant arrangement is made more unusual by adding pretty paper, such as giftwrap, to long stemmed roses. It will work particularly well on a narrow shelf or mantelpiece.

1 Using a high-sided narrow tank like the one shown, cut a block of wet florist's foam to fit inside. Make sure the foam comes at least halfway up the tank as this will support the rose stems.

2 Depending on the size of the tank, take three or four long stemmed roses and cut them so that they are long enough to stand high above the tank and go to the base. Remove all leaves and thorns from the stems.

3 Take the paper and cut a strip for each stem, about two or three inches wide. Make four or five slits in the paper several centimetres apart. Thread the paper onto the stems, move the paper up the stems and place them a few inches apart in the tank. Finally arrange the paper into waves on the stems.

Flowers used in photography:
long stemmed green roses

Ivy tray

This is an interesting way of using a low dish or tray which has been made to look very attractive by combining texture and colour.

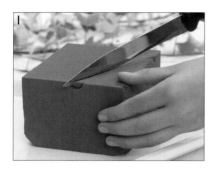

1 Use a block of florist's wet foam which is about 10cm thick and cut it to roughly the shape of your tray or dish. Leave plenty of room around the sides so the foam doesn't touch the edges. If the tray is big you may find that you will need two blocks of foam taped together.

2 Now make a well in the centre of the foam, about 5cm in diameter. Soak the foam in water. Use trailing ivy and push the cut ends into the foam around the well. Wind it around the block of foam, continue to do this until the foam is covered.

3 Finally fill the well with flowers. They need to be cut to a height that is just above the height of the foam. Use varieties such as narcissus, sweet William or for Christmas you could try bunches of berries.

Flowers used in photography:
variegated ivy, heather

Roman fantasy

Looking out for unusual containers is part of the fun about creating flower arrangements. This is just such a piece; originally a container for the garden, with a little imagination this makes a stunning indoor flower display.

1 Place a glass bowl into the top of the pedestal and fill it with florist's foam. Alternatively, you could make a wire mesh to fit the bowl.

2 Cover the foam or mesh with a layer of moss. Pick flowers with rich colours and exotic looks. Try using hostas for their large leaves and other unusual flowers such as protea.

3 Start by using trailing greenery and place groups of them around the sides, not all areas need to be filled as you want to get a nice, flowing look. Start to build the centre of the piece by grouping the flowers by type, not too much height is needed here, just a good variety of colours and textures.

Flowers used in photography: amaranthus, ivy, wild angelica, hydrangea, lisianthus, moss

Space tank flowers

A cool and contemporary look has been achieved here by displaying flowers within the confines of a glass tank.

1 Choose a glass tank of any size, as long as the flowers you are using will fit inside it. Varieties like alliums, agapanthus, nerines and most orchids will work well for this display. Make sure the tank is sparkling clean by polishing it inside and out.

2 Place some clean gravel or glass beads in the bottom of the tank, this will need to be a couple of centimetres deep in order to hold the flowers in place. Now cover the gravel or beads with water.

3 Choose strong bold shapes for the flowers which will look graphic behind the glass. Cut the flowers to fit within the confines of the tank and arrange to make a bold shape, placing the stems into the gravel to hold them in place.

Flowers used in photography:
alliums, globe thistle

Acknowledgements

I would like to thank my sister Geraldine and her family for use of their lovely house for the photoshoots for the book. The author and publishers would also like to thank the following shop for their assistance in supplying the props that were used in this book:

The Pier
200 Tottenham Court Road
London W1T 7PL
Tel: 0207 637 7001
www.pier.co.uk